Original title:
A Brooch of Power

Copyright © 2025 Creative Arts Management OÜ
All rights reserved.

Author: Colin Leclair
ISBN HARDBACK: 978-1-80586-178-2
ISBN PAPERBACK: 978-1-80586-650-3

The Unfurling Legacy

In a drawer with dust galore,
Lies a pin that I adore.
It sparkles bright with every glance,
A true contender in the dance.

With quirks and charms, it struts about,
A fashionista with a shout.
It claims the title, 'Fashion King',
But really, it can't do a thing.

People laugh and raise an eye,
When it winks and gives a sigh.
It tries to shine, but what a flop,
Held together by a single drop.

Yet on my chest, it holds its ground,
Making merry, twirls around.
A legacy of flair, oh dear,
This comical gem brings us cheer.

Beacon of Brilliance

Oh what a sight, a shiny pin,
That claims to be my fashion twin.
It glows with flair, like big parade,
Yet feigned elegance, it's just a charade.

At gatherings, it likes to boast,
Of parties too wild, it loves to toast.
But wait! What's that beneath the light?
A hint of glue, a silly fright!

Worn sideways, it's a comedic twist,
A broach of laughs, you can't resist.
With pals around, we laugh and cheer,
This beacon of fun, the star of the sphere.

From bumbling nights to clever tricks,
It leads us on with goofy picks.
Oh, poke me gently,
don't let it sway,
For brilliance is best in a quirky way!

The Charm of Unyielding Spirit

In a pocket tucked tight,
Lies a gem of pure delight.
With a wink and a spin,
It's sure to make you grin.

When the world feels quite rough,
This charm says, 'You've got stuff!'
It bounces back with style,
Making life a little more guile.

Threads of Destiny

In a fabric so bright,
Lies destiny's bite.
Sewn with laughter and cheer,
It whispers, 'Have no fear!'

Twists and turns we embrace,
As we dance in this race.
With every stitch we laugh,
We're editing the path.

Adornments of Legacy

Worn by someone who's wise,
With a gleam in their eyes.
These trinkets tell a tale,
Of adventures set sail.

Each layer holds a jest,
In jest, they truly invest.
Legacy's comedic flair,
A dance of joy to share.

The Glimmer of Control

With a flick and a twist,
It commands like a mist.
A sparkle in the air,
Says, 'Oh, do you dare?'

In a world that spins mad,
This glimmer's always glad.
With a chuckle, it steals,
The power that reveals.

The Guardian's Gem

In the cloak of a wizard, it gleams bright,
A guardian's giggle, a comical sight.
It sparkles with mischief, breaks all the rules,
Making wise men forget their big, golden jewels.

On the chest of a knight, it feels like a prank,
At each silly jest, his courage is blank.
With magical laughter, it dances around,
A gem of confusion, the silliest found.

The Brooch of Destiny

Intended for greatness, yet stuck on a hat,
This little gem thinks it's far more than that.
It whispers to the wearer, 'You'll be quite grand!',
But the only thing growing is dust on the stand.

A destiny draped in a fabric of fun,
It sparkles and giggles, when the day is done.
Flip a coin for choices, let it decide,
But don't be surprised if you end up fried!

The Monarch's Tribute

On a robe of a monarch, it shines like a star,
Yet it wiggles and jigs, like a jazz guitar.
With each royal bow, there's a sway and a spin,
To keep up its charm, it must always grin.

A tribute to fashion, a pinch of absurd,
It snorts when it sparkles, such laughter is heard.
Command the respect, the laughter's no fault,
For rulership's heavy, but that's how it's taught!

Scepter in Miniature

A tiny scepter waves, full of flair,
In a tiny hand, waving left, waving air.
It's all quite majestic in looking the part,
But it trips on its nose, and that's just the start.

With a flick and a twirl, it proudly presents,
A laughable dance with regal pretense.
Though might be small, it commands all the cheer,
In the kingdom of laughter, it holds court right here!

Tokens of Tenacity

In a world where socks misplace,
A mismatched pair has found its grace.
With colors bright, they strut about,
Defying odds, they laugh and shout.

A paperclip holds tight its dream,
While others rust, it finds its gleam.
In boardroom battles, it wears a crown,
Who knew office supplies could take the town?

The chewing gum, a trusty friend,
Memory lane, it helps to mend.
Stuck to shoes or under chairs,
It brings us smiles, tries not to scare.

With buttons bold, we make our stand,
A comic touch, so unplanned.
In every wardrobe, they play their part,
Fashion humor, a work of art.

Echoes of Elegance

A feather duster waves with pride,
Dancing in corners, it must confide.
Tickling dust, it pirouettes,
With sparks of joy, it never sweats.

A sassy spoon in the drawer stays,
Whispering secrets of silver days.
It stirs up laughter with every scoop,
Who knew cutlery could form a troupe?

A lipstick tube rolls with flair,
Brushing colors in the air.
It narrates tales of first dates bright,
Creating smiles, a pure delight.

A muffin tin's a rugged knight,
Baking wonders, oh what a sight!
With crumbs and laughter, it takes its bow,
In this kitchen, we thrive somehow.

Gilded Essence

A quirky pin upon the chest,
Declares each day a charming quest.
With sparkles that refuse to fade,
It winks at life, unafraid.

A vintage key that unlocks the fun,
It tells old tales 'til day is done.
Jangling cheer in every nook,
"Oh look, here comes the jovial crook!"

The rubber band, a stretch so grand,
Supporting mischief, so well planned.
It snaps with glee when tensions rise,
A playful spirit that never lies.

A bottle cap sits noble and round,
With tales of parties, laughter found.
As it rolls away, it leaves its charm,
In every heart, no need for alarm.

Charmed against the Storm

An umbrella bright with polka dots,
Defies the rain, it simply trots.
Twirls against puddles, a dance so spry,
Fending off raindrops with a winked eye.

A raincoat clad in vibrant hues,
Makes gloomy days feel like a cruise.
Turning storms into shows of glee,
It grins, it laughs, it's wild and free.

The galoshes jump in puddles deep,
With splashes soaring, it's quite a leap!
Each squishy step, a joyful cheer,
Who knew walking wet could bring such cheer?

A wind-up toy soldiers in parade,
Marching through tempest; never afraid.
With every wobble, they steal the show,
In storms of life, let laughter flow.

Charmed Resilience

In a pocket snug, it plays,
With mischief in its gleaming gaze.
A tiny guardian on my chest,
Making bad days seem the best.

It whispers jokes throughout the day,
Winking as it leads the way.
With a flick and a flash, it's sure to say,
"Let's dance our worries all away!"

As I strut with newfound grace,
It smiles bright in its proper place.
The world may frown, but it just beams,
Turning mundane into wild dreams.

Oh, sparkle with your cheeky grin,
Together we will always win.
In every laugh, we find our flow,
With charm so bright, we steal the show.

Unveiling the Hidden Force

Beneath the layers, laughter grows,
A secret force that nobody knows.
It tickles minds with silly cheer,
Turning gloom to giggles near.

When troubles knock, it takes a stance,
Dancing lightly, it leads the chance.
With a wink and a sly little turn,
It teaches joy, oh how we learn!

In quirky styles, it claims its right,
Adding spice to every night.
This playful charm, a force of fun,
With it, my days are never done!

Through every prank and jesting game,
Life's a stage, and it's to blame.
With laughter loud and smiles wide,
This hidden force, my joyful guide.

Motifs of Might

From fabrics woven, bold and bright,
A quirky spark ignites the night.
With colors loud and patterns proud,
It struts its stuff beneath the crowd.

Fortunes twist with every glance,
Unlikely heroes in a dance.
With cheeky charm, they take the floor,
In playful jest, they roar for more.

Each motif tells a laugh-filled tale,
As giggles ride like a merry gale.
This tapestry of whimsical art,
Finds ways to tickle every heart.

So wear your colors, loud and free,
Join in the fun, come dance with me!
In a world that's dressed in grey,
Let's stitch our joy into the day!

Glinting with Purpose

A sparkly wink upon my gaze,
Sparks a joy that brightly sways.
Glimmers tease with every flip,
Ready for their playful trip.

With purpose bold, yet fun galore,
They burst with laughter, never bore.
In playful dance, they steal the moon,
Singing sweetly, a silly tune.

Every shimmer tells a jest,
Joyful hearts put to the test.
With each twinkle, a tale unfolds,
Of humor worth more than gold.

So let them scatter, let them shine,
In this wacky world, they intertwine.
With glints of joy, and smiles to share,
Life's a carnival, and we're the flair!

The Atlas's Jewel

In a pocket, it bumbles, quite proud,
A shiny thing, gathers every crowd.
It thinks it's fierce, a cape, a crown,
But really, it just keeps falling down.

With maps that seem to go awry,
It leads us where the tacos lie.
"Oh look, it's pointing to a tree!"
"Isn't that where our snack should be?"

We pin it on with hope and flair,
Yet off it flops, without a care.
And when it glimmers in the sun,
It winks and giggles—oh, what fun!

"Let's take a selfie, say cheese loud!"
But it distracts and steals the crowd.
A tiny gem of mischief found,
In adventures, it's forever bound.

Herald of Hope

On my jacket proudly pinned,
It swirls and twirls like a comic wind.
With glitter that just won't sit still,
It sparkles with a willful thrill.

"Look over there!" it seems to shout,
As if it's got some special route.
Yet all it does is make folks stare,
As it flutters in the summer air.

Sometimes it thinks it's a wise sage,
With stories straight from the grandest age.
But instead, it just makes us laugh,
We'd much prefer a stylish gaffe.

And when we're lost, it takes its stand,
With clumsy confidence, it's rather grand.
Oh, herald of cheer, with stories to weave,
As long as you're here, we'll never grieve.

The Illuminated Badge

In the gloom, it shines like a star,
Yet in my pocket, it's gone too far.
"It glows at night!" I proudly claim,
While searching for it, what a game!

It darts and dances, seeking attention,
With no sense of direction or convention.
People laugh as it leads us astray,
Like a disco ball in bright sunlight's ray.

Attached to my coat with care and pride,
It gives me giggles, takes me for a ride.
"Is that a badge or a cooking pan?"
"It's meant to dazzle, don't you understand?"

So here I stroll with this lighted charm,
Though it's mostly just a reason to disarm.
And on this wild adventure we'll forge,
A glowing friendship, forever in charge!

The Everbright Brooch

Oh, what a gem, so bold and bright,
It boasts of magic and reveals delight.
Yet in its glimmer, it hides a prank,
A fashion faux pas, a whimsical flank.

"Oh look, it's like a shooting star!"
But wait till it dangles too far.
It flaps and flops, always in the way,
"Did you mean to wear it like that today?"

At parties, it struts with all its glee,
Declaring itself as royalty.
Yet I can't help but laugh so loud,
For it's the crown of the silly crowd.

In sunlight, it twinkles with a flare,
"Let's take a picture! I'll be a rare air!"
So here we are, my crooked friend,
Together in laughter, until the end.

The Prestige Pendant

In a world of shimmer and shine,
A pendant danced, quite divine.
It swung from the neck of a pompous king,
Yet whispered secrets of a chicken wing.

With each twirl, it made a sound,
Like giggles echoing all around.
The courtiers laughed, but none could see,
The royal jester's grand decree.

He claimed this trinket held great might,
But still lost to a kid in a fight.
The power was sheer, for laughter spread,
With each silly joke the jester said.

Oh, this charm on the king's noble chest,
Brought mirth and glee, not a royal jest.
And thus they ruled, with joy unbound,
A king and his jester, both silly and sound.

Mantle of Majesty

A mantle draped with flair and zeal,
Proclaimed itself a royal deal.
But every time it went for a sweep,
It sent the monarch into a heap.

The fabric shone, a dazzling hue,
Yet tangled up like a cat with glue.
With each grand gesture, a trip or fall,
Made the subjects giggle at the royal sprawl.

The king declared he wore it proud,
While the villagers roared, oh so loud.
For every twist, a pratfall or two,
A comedy show, and not a royal view.

He'd strut and preen, with confidence rife,
But the mantle led him to a comical life.
And in this chuckle fest of a court,
The kingdom laughed, a merry sport.

The Warden's Wreath

A wreath of greens, with blossoms bright,
Claimed to bestow a guardian's might.
Yet as he wore it, oh what a sight,
It perched like a bird, ready for flight.

The warden stood, so brave and tall,
But tripped on his not-so-manly shawl.
The flowers chuckled, as he hit the ground,
While frogs nearby leaped and abound.

He shooed the critters with a frown,
But they continued their joyous sound.
For every stomp, a bounce, a jest,
Made all the creatures feel so blessed.

Thus he abandoned the solemn pose,
Adopted dance moves like a wild rose.
In laughter's grip, he learned to believe,
That even in guarding, one could achieve.

Diadem of Destiny

A diadem sparkled on a queen's brow,
Promising fate with every vow.
Yet on a crown, it gave a jest,
It slipped and sent her pal off west!

With gems that twinkled in such a show,
It sparkled so bright, yet choreographed woe.
Each royal ball turned into a dance,
While the crown tumbled down at chance!

The queen declared, with laughter anew,
"I'm destined to rule, but so are you!"
As nobles rallied, weathering the spins,
These coat-tails of fate led to comical wins.

Thus in the kingdom where giggles reigned,
A shiny crown kept the pure entertained.
For even amidst a regal decree,
Laughter stood gifted, wild, and free.

The Empowering Flame

In a land of long-forgotten lore,
A spark ignites, as laughter roars.
A tiny trinket, shiny and bright,
Turns grumpy frowns into pure delight.

With each twinkle, a giggle's released,
It feeds on joys, never on yeast.
A dash of wit, a sprinkle of cheer,
This flickering light chases off fear.

Wear it proudly, a badge of jest,
In silly moments, we are all blessed.
The flame of fun, forever to keep,
In our hearts, it runs deep.

So let the fire of laughter blaze,
In mundane life, start a craze.
With every chortle, spirits will rise,
Unseen magic hides in disguise.

The Fortune's Emblem

A doodad pinning good luck's tune,
Worn with style, not just a boon.
It wiggles as you dance with flair,
Tickles timid souls unaware.

A wiggly charm for those who dare,
To mix up snacks, or fly through air.
It brings the giggles, spins around,
Turns quiet days to joy profound.

With lollipop colors, it can't go wrong,
In every wink, find a silly song.
Not merely fortune, but fun encapsulated,
In a world where laughter's celebrated.

So don this symbol with a cheeky grin,
Let happiness swirl and twirl within.
For in this charm, the bright rays play,
And silly squirrels leap into the fray.

Haven of Hope

In a pocket of laughter, safe and sound,
Lies a treasure of whims, joy knows no bound.
Adorned with giggles, it welcomes all,
Whispers of hope when shadows call.

Each time you frown, just reach inside,
This tiny haven, your trusty guide.
It tugs at smiles like gentle strings,
Unleashing butterflies, on vibrant wings.

When life throws pies, or silly pranks,
This emblem forms your jester ranks.
With every glance, light ignites,
In the weirdest times, joy ignites.

Riding the waves of whimsy and cheer,
In laughter's harbor, there's nothing to fear.
So toast to the moments, let giggles awaken,
In this space of joy, never mistaken.

The Ascendant Jewel

A gem so bright, it might just glow,
Bringing laughter in a witty flow.
Not for riches, but for smiles dear,
It's the silliest thing you want near.

In moments dark, it leads the way,
With tangled tongues, and playful sway.
It jinks and jives, a brave little star,
Taking you places both near and far.

When troubles come, this jewel will jive,
Spinning tales where laughter thrives.
A quirky spark, in times of blur,
Your goofy guide, so miles ahead it'll stir.

So clasp this bauble, let it shine,
In crazed adventures, you'll be just fine.
For as you wear this trinket, dear,
Life's loops will twirl with effortless cheer.

Glimmer of Governance

In a kingdom where laughter reigns,
The jewels whisper silly refrains.
A crown made of tinfoil and dreams,
Governance bursts at the seams.

Rulers dance in polka-dot shoes,
Swaying to tunes of the silliest blues.
The orb is a beach ball, they toss—
Who knew ruling could lead to such loss!

Each decree, a joke with a twist,
Making court jesters clench their fists.
But laughter is mighty, or so they say,
When the scepter's just a big bouquet.

So here's to the reign of giggles and cheer,
Where power is simply a joke, my dear.
And as long as the laughter's around,
In silliness, true strength can be found.

The Radiant Regalia

In a palace decked in sparkle and light,
A robe made of sequins shines oh-so-bright.
The throne is a beanbag, plush and round,
Where kings and queens bounce without making a sound.

Dressing for power, they wear silly hats,
Feathers and glitter, adorned like cats.
The sceptre's a rubber chicken, fierce and bold,
Power's a show, or so they're told.

With laughter echoing down the grand hall,
Regalia that trips at the slightest fall.
The feast is a picnic, with ketchup galore,
As subjects all giggle and call for more!

So if you seek power, embrace the jest,
It's the chuckles that truly prove best.
In this dazzling attire, where humor's the key,
Ruling with laughter? That's how it should be!

Keeper of the Flame

There once was a keeper with jokes up her sleeve,
With a flick of the wrist, would light up, believe!
Her flame was a candle, shaped like a clown,
Lighting up laughter all over the town.

In her whimsical chamber where nothing made sense,
The walls were all mirrors—a path quite intense.
To rule from a throne of balloons and cheer,
Was to keep her kingdom free from all fear.

With flames turning colors, like sprinkles on cake,
She'd giggle and wiggle, a powerful quake.
The secret to strength? A snooze or a show,
For power is silly, just let it all flow!

So remember this keeper, brightening days,
With her laughter-lit flame, the silliest ways.
The kingdom may giggle, with joy in their hearts,
For the keeper of fun, true power imparts.

The Silvered Sigil

A silvered sigil, so shiny and loud,
With a wink and a grin, it drew in a crowd.
The emblem of power, yet quite the surprise,
A face that just giggles, and rolls its eyes.

Worn by a ruler who can't stop to chat,
Flipping through jokes faster than the cat.
Each scroll is a riddle, a giggle-filled mess,
In a world where the serious simply guess.

With banners of cupcakes and ice-cream galore,
Declarations that leave them all wanting more.
The silver shines bright, but it's laughter that gleams,
In the kingdom of chuckles, where joy reigns supreme.

So strap on the sigil, go dance in the street,
With fun as the motto, life's always a treat!
In a world full of whimsy and brave silly feats,
This is the power that truly competes.

Radiant Resilience

It sparkled bright upon her chest,
A badge of honor, quite the jest.
With every glance, it swayed and shone,
Who knew such bling could claim a throne?

The power posed in its light twist,
Even the cat felt it couldn't resist.
With sequins dancing, much to declare,
It fought off gloom with a glittering flare.

A laugh erupted from every jewel,
As it schooled all in the art of cool.
So when life gets heavy, just take a chance,
And let that sparkle lead the dance!

For who needs crowns or swords to wield,
When shiny things might just reveal?
True strength lies not in swords or might,
But in a bling that glimmers bright!

Adornment of Authority

Upon his coat, a gem so grand,
It whispered secrets, not as planned.
With every nod, it seemed to show,
Who really ran this quirky show.

He strutted in, with flair and pride,
And all around felt vertigo ride.
That sparkly thing had quite the pull,
Making him think he was so cool.

The meetings turned to raucous roars,
As that adornment opened doors.
"Who's in charge?" the crowd would say,
"The one with bling, hip-hip-hooray!"

And thus, the tale goes on and on,
Of a man with gems who thought he shone.
But mostly it was laughter, bright,
From a silly brooch that stole the night!

Gemstone of Influence

In a dull meeting, the clock ticked slow,
But there on the table, a gem would glow.
With winks and smiles, it led the way,
Turning yawns into fun, come what may!

"Just look at this stone!" someone did brag,
As eyes were drawn, like moths to a snag.
"It's the key to power!" they all did cheer,
While sipping coffee, with donuts near.

It sparked ideas, wild and free,
That unlocked wisdom—oh, what a spree!
From prompts of laughter to grins so wide,
The gemstone ruled, a whimsical guide.

So if you seek to change the game,
Just flaunt some bling and stake your claim.
For in this life, the truth can't hide,
The real influence rests in your pride!

The Chancellor's Charm

The Chancellor sauntered with quite the flair,
A glimmering piece that turned every stare.
With each tense debate, it sparkled and shone,
Unlocking laughter in every tone.

"Oh look, it's bling that seals the deal!"
They whispered and giggled, sharing the feel.
From boring scripts to jokes all around,
The humor ignited, our hope unbound.

What power it wielded, a secret untold,
Turning the cold to warmth, and bold.
Every shuffle of papers, a whimsical dance,
As the Chancellor's charm led all to prance!

So here's to the days of left and right,
When robes and gems made laughter bright.
For rules may bend, but smiles will remain,
With a little sparkle, no need for disdain!

Mirror of Might

In the chest it gleams with flair,
A shiny charm that seems quite rare.
It winks at me with a funny grin,
Whispers secrets to let the fun begin.

With every glance, I puff my chest,
Feeling like I'm simply the best.
It gives me courage, or so I claim,
To dance like a fool without any shame.

Crest of the Conqueror

Upon my shirt, it sits so proud,
A little crest that draws a crowd.
I strut around like a royal fool,
Pretending I'm still in high school.

The label says 'conqueror' bright,
But really, I just want a bite.
It's just a badge, but oh, what fun,
I wear it like I've already won!

The Connective Gem

Oh, the gem that links us all,
It's sparkly, shiny, and not too small.
When I wear it, friends gather near,
Laughing at jokes I pretend to hear.

It binds our hearts, or so they say,
But mainly it's just here to play.
With every jingle, it pulls a laugh,
Making old tales seem like a gaffe.

The Pinnacle of Grace

Nestled above, a twinkling star,
I swear it's traveled from afar.
It's the pinnacle, or so they cheer,
While I say, "It's just a souvenir!"

With every step, I feel quite grand,
Though it's just plastic from a stand.
But hey, it's fun to wear with glee,
As long as it makes them laugh at me!

The Shielded Treasure

In pockets deep, it hides away,
A glint of mischief, here to stay.
It dazzles minds, and grabs a glance,
A treasure small, that loves to dance.

With every twist, it steals the show,
An ally of the brave, you know.
Worn at a party, it takes the lead,
A crafty gem, with laughter to feed.

It whispers tales of daring quests,
Of silly fights, and jesters' tests.
A sparkling wink, a cheeky grin,
Unveiling fun, thick as a pin.

So if you seek a wild delight,
This shining charm makes wrong feel right.
Wear it with glee, embrace the jest,
For in its glow, you'll feel the best.

Radiance of Resolve

On lapels bold, it takes a stand,
A cheeky spark, a playful brand.
When battles loom and frowns set in,
This tiny gem will always win.

With every twinkle, it starts a cheer,
Fetching smiles from far and near.
Jokes and puns, the perfect match,
A shiny friend, no need to hatch.

It fuels the fire when spirits wane,
A gem that dances through the rain.
A laugh, a jig, and off we'll go,
With dainty threads, we steal the show.

In every heart, it plants some zest,
Invoking giggles, that's its quest.
Twirling wildly, the night is ours,
This spark of life, our guiding stars.

The Commanding Spark

Amidst the crowd, it takes a bow,
With quirky style, it says, "Look now!"
A tiny crown upon the lapel,
Where joy explodes and giggles dwell.

It flickers bright, demands a laugh,
A shiny jest, its better half.
As chatter fills the room with cheer,
The cheeky glint draws everyone near.

Each glance it catches, a lively thrill,
A charm that bends the fates at will.
From silly pranks to belly rolls,
A spark of fun, ignites our souls.

"Wear me well!" it seems to sing,
As laughter echoes, hearts take wing.
For in this gem, we find our flair,
A rallying cry, a party's air.

Jewel of the Dawn

At sunrise's glow, it catches light,
With morning whimsy, it's pure delight.
A shining laugh in sunlight's tease,
This gem of fun brings all to ease.

With every sparkle, a story starts,
Of wild adventures, and merry hearts.
It jokes with shadows, tickles the day,
Dancing through moments, come what may.

It whispers secrets of joy and grace,
A mischief-maker in every space.
Adorning smiles, it claims its throne,
A jewel of jests, we call our own.

So as the daylight paints the skies,
This playful charm, we won't disguise.
For in its shine, we find our song,
A laughter gem, where we belong.

Light of the Loyal

In a drawer, it resides, so bold,
With secrets and tales that never grow old.
Sparkling bright in the soft morning light,
It whispers of charm, of joy, and delight.

Oh, the pets it attracts with just a small gleam,
Cats think it's a toy, in all honesty, a dream!
But peg that on me, and watch them all stop,
For this shining small gem is the ultimate prop.

Friendship's warm glow on my chest does appear,
It laughs as I fumble and spill all my beer.
With each clink and clatter, a shimmery dance,
It's a party, it says! Come on, take a chance!

So here's to the sparkle that brings us together,
Through mishaps and giggles, like birds of a feather.
Hold tight to your treasures, let none slip away,
A gem full of laughter brightens the day!

The Questing Quasar

In the night sky, the glimmer appears,
A quest from the cosmos that tickles my ears.
A shiny small orb with dreams on the run,
It pulls at my heart like a joke under sun.

In search of a hero, it raises a brow,
'Who'll wear me with pride? Come take a bow!'
I tried on my cat, who took off in fright,
This cosmic accessory couldn't be more bright.

We wandered through galaxies, danced with the stars,
But my friends thought I was just playing with cars.
"Oh please, it's important!" I said with a grin,
Who knew space adventures began with a pin?

So we laughed through the void, aiming high with each jest,
A cosmic caper that brought out the best.
And if you see shimmer in the dark up above,
It's just me and my quasar, spreading the love!

Orb of Ambition

On my sleeve, it spins tales of goals so grand,
A orb full of hopes in a whimsical hand.
It rolls and it wobbles, a jester's delight,
Chasing all dreams with a quirky invite.

What's this? An idea? A whim, just a spark!
With this shiny round charm, I'm ready to embark.
To conquer the world with a bounce in my stride,
Daring each challenge, I'll never subside.

People laugh at my antics, my plans, so absurd,
But they'll learn in the end, I have the last word.
"Just look at my orb!" I declare with a flair,
"It knows all the secrets, the wonders out there!"

So here's to ambition with a twinkle and twist,
With each little wobble, how could I resist?
The journey is wild, with laughter and cheer,
I'll wear this round gem, it makes dreams crystal clear!

The Phoenix's Pin

From ashes it came, a flicker of fun,
A pin for the brave and the bold, not to shun.
With wings made of laughter, it's ready to soar,
Signaling mischief, who could ask for more?

It grins as I strut with my head held so high,
A little reminder that even I can fly.
On my lapel bright, it sparks endless cheer,
"This life is a party, so come on, my dear!"

I prance like a phoenix, in coats of bright hues,
With quirky old humor that always renews.
Friends gather 'round, under the dazzling sun,
"For laughs and for giggles, this pin's number one!"

So let's toast to the laughter, the flight, and the fun,
To the spark of the phoenix, on journeys begun.
With joy in our hearts and this pin as our guide,
We'll rise up together, in laughter and pride!

Talisman of Triumph

In the depths of my jacket, it sits quite proud,
A shiny little gem, drawing quite a crowd.
It claims to bring luck, always says it's true,
But I tripped over air while wearing the view.

With magical sparkles that dazzle the eyes,
The moment I wear it, I feel like the prize.
Yet when dinner's served, it flies off the plate,
And I'm left with the crumbs, oh, what a fate!

Friends ask for wisdom, I'll roll it out wide,
"A gem of great fortune!" they cheer with great pride.
But it whispers to me, as I sip on my tea,
"Just don't talk to strangers, or you're in for a spree!"

In the end, I've embraced this quirky delight,
With laughter and giggles, it shines in the light.
If fortune's a gamble, I'm rolling the dice,
With a wink and a chuckle, who needs to think twice!

Threads of Fortitude

Tangled in fabric, it holds my defenses,
A swirl of bright colors, over the expenses.
Believing it's magic, I wear with great glee,
But it laughs when I slip on a banana peel spree.

It claims it has powers, it's sewn with great care,
Yet it snags on the wallpaper, oh, what a snare!
When asked about troubles, it always will joke,
Yet the stitch on my sleeve looks ready to choke.

Worn on my collar, it brightens the day,
It hops like a frog when I dance and sway.
And when people gawk, I just laugh with the thread,
"Don't mind me, I'm fancy—just look at my head!"

As days turn to weeks, it's still here for the ride,
With mismatched flamboyance, my joy and my pride.
If laughter's the treasure, I've struck gold for sure,
In these whimsical threads, let the fun endure!

Secrets Worn Upon the Soul

Nestled on my lapel, it grins with a wink,
Whispers of secrets, but I can't even think.
It nudges my heart like a playful little sprite,
As I trip on my tongue during casual bites.

A symbol of stories, both strange and absurd,
It tells of adventures with nary a word.
Should I take it off? Or just rock the embrace?
It's a wise little feather, a curious face!

As I stroll through the park, it seems to shout out,
"Shall we tease those pigeons? Come on, let's pout!"
And sure enough, chaos ensues on the scene,
With laughter echoing, my carefree routine.

So, here I am wearing this jester-like charm,
It brings zest to my outfits, keeps me from harm.
In this world of blandness, I'll flaunt my bright role,
With secrets aplenty, won't hide my whole soul!

The Enigma in the Pin

It glints like a riddle, a puzzle of fun,
On days I'm feeling lazy or basking in sun.
With each twist and turn, it knows how to play,
But sometimes it's cunning; it runs the odd way.

A pointy little sprite, with a wink and a grin,
It causes pretend chaos, yet calls me a win.
When I face my opponents, with flair and a jest,
It spins tales of glory, making me feel blessed.

Dressed for success, I prance down the street,
When someone asks, "What's that?" I jump to my feet.
"Oh, just a little trinket!" I giggle and tease,
It giggles back softly, "I'll do what I please!"

Unraveled, it whispers great treasures untold,
With a flair for the humorous and fortunes of old.
In this playful affair, I'm a part of the jest,
A radiant enigma; I'm truly the best!

Pendant of Potency

I wore a charm that looked so bright,
It whispered secrets deep at night.
But when I sneezed, oh what a sight,
It turned my cat into a kite!

With jewels that sparkle, I felt so grand,
Yet all my friends just laughed and planned.
They took my charm, it slipped like sand,
And now the toaster's in a band!

I tried to cook some toast one day,
But ended up in a ballet!
My kitchen danced, a grand display,
Now popcorn flies like it's on a sleigh!

But through the madness, I will wear,
This quirky piece with stories rare.
For laughter's magic, none compare,
To the joy within a jester's flair.

The Crystal Conductor

In my pocket, a shiny stone,
It bobs and weaves, a little moan.
Turned my dog into a drone,
Now he buzzes with a happy tone!

It led the squirrels to tap dance well,
Creating quite the woodland spell.
But the neighbors rang my bell,
Inquiring why mice now all dwell.

I tried to use it for my art,
But it transformed my brush to dart.
Now every canvas plays a part,
As it turns into a wild chart!

My crystal giggles, crystal sings,
It's better than most simpler things.
Embracing all the chaos it brings,
I'm just here laughing at my flings!

Enchantment in Elegance

In a boutique, I found a flair,
A sparkle caught me unaware.
A twirl of fabric, quite a dare,
It ended up on my pet bear!

Posh parties called for grand display,
But my charm made everyone sway.
As hats flew high, what a ballet,
Now every head has gone astray!

I thought I'd charm the local queen,
But it turned my toast to a guillotine.
I laughed so hard, I lost my sheen,
While trying on a dress routine.

In elegance, I'm less aloof,
Each stumble just adds to my proof.
That magic mischief, can be goofed,
A joyous heart is the best hoof!

Starlit Sovereignty

A crown of stars, oh what a sight,
It made my head require a flight.
I reigned for days, with all my might,
Until I tripped on sheer delight!

With royal pomp, I waved my hand,
But suddenly, the cows did stand.
They mooed and danced, oh isn't it grand?
My scepter turned into a band!

I sipped my tea, as all went wild,
While birds sang tunes, and 'twas beguiled.
A sparkly cloak, quite meek and mild,
Brought charming chaos, oh so styled!

Yet joy reigns supreme in this realm,
Funny tales help us at the helm.
In starlit nights, we all can overwhelm,
And laughter sits upon the whelm!

Gems of the Heart

A sparkling stone on my chest,
My friends all jest, they think it's the best.
A flashy relic with a silly clue,
No one can guess what it really can do.

With every twinkle, it tells a tall tale,
Of where I've been and the mischief I sail.
It's magic, they say, but they just roll their eyes,
As I wink at the ladies and won their surprise.

Each gem holds secrets of long-lost cheer,
Like why I dance in my colorful gear.
And when it glimmers, it leads to a laugh,
Just ask my cat, he'll give you the graph.

So if you see me, just know I'm quite clever,
With jewels that shine and jokes that last forever.
In this life of ours, let's wear the bizarre,
For laughter and joy are the true shining stars.

Adornment of Authority

With a shiny pin, I strut down the lane,
Claiming power like a ruler—in vain.
My friends all snicker, they know it's a joke,
But I wear this thing like a knight's heavy cloak.

"Who's the boss?" I huff with regal flair,
While tripping on shoes and tangling my hair.
The more I parade, the more laughter erupts,
For wisdom, you see, is best served in cups.

It might be a trinket, yet I'm feeling grand,
Waving it proudly, I take a bold stand.
Like a cat on a throne, I declare with delight,
"Banish your worries, I'm ruling tonight!"

With laughter my scepter and giggles my crown,
I reign over chuckles in this quirky town.
So if you've a bauble you want to parade,
Just wear it with pride, and let joy invade.

Elegance Forged in Strength

In a world of glam, I found my true voice,
A flashy pin offers me a wild choice.
I strut like a gladiator covered in gold,
While my mom just sighs, "How can you be bold?"

This treasure I cling to, all shiny and bright,
It defies the storm, like a beacon of light.
But watch your step, for I'm catching some stars,
In a place where elegance meets jovial bars.

Each twinkle empowers my wobbly feet,
As I dance like a squirrel, can't keep a straight beat.
Yet dignity whispers from crannies of fun,
With laughter my armor, let's go on the run!

So join me, dear friend, take a chance on the dance,
With this quirky adornment, let's give joy a chance.
Elegance shines when we let laughter reign,
And the strength of our hearts breaks free of the chain.

Emblems of Enchantment

Behold! A token of whimsical might,
Worn on my jacket, it sparkles so bright.
A dragon or maybe just a spud,
Who would have thought it could cause such a flood?

"Is that a real gem?" the skeptics all ponder,
As I twirl and twist in a dance full of wonder.
With each little flick, it casts a wild spell,
Even the squirrels join, ringing their bell.

This charm is my charm, it opens the door,
To the laughter of friends—who could ask for more?
So let's toast to the chaos this bauble creates,
Where enchantment and humor are mingling with fate.

Widget be widget, it doesn't make sense,
But leave all the logic—let's be a bit tense!
For in every spark lies a tale yet untold,
And together we'll wear it, both goofy and bold.

Token of Triumph

In the pocket it lay, quite proud,
A shiny little thing, amidst the crowd.
It winked at me with a cheeky jest,
'Why not wear me? I'm the very best!'

I clasped it on, feeling quite bold,
It whispered secrets of legends of old.
Yet every time I tried to impress,
It slipped and fell – oh, what a mess!

The squirrels around, they let out a cheer,
'Look at that fool, he's lost his rear!'
But I laughed along, true power's a jest,
With laughter and chaos, I was truly blessed!

So here's to the trinkets that sparkle and gleam,
They may not be magic, but they fuel the dream.
A token of triumph, or so they call,
Let joy be the treasure, the greatest of all!

The Fierce Amulet

Oh, behold the fierce charm, hung 'round my neck,
It promises strength but still feels like a wreck.
One tug from the cat, and I'm sent for a spin,
Flipping over in laughter, where do I begin?

A knight in my yard once came to my door,
Claiming this talisman deserved to soar.
He tripped on a flower, fell flat on his face,
'This amulet's potent!' he yelled as he paced.

I strut like a peacock, bold in my stance,
Yet with every misstep, I look like a dance.
'Fear not!' I declare, 'for I've courage galore!'
Yet I trip on my shoelace and tumble once more.

With each little mishap, I rally and cheer,
Embracing the chaos, 'tis magic, I fear!
So here's to the amulets, fierce and unkempt,
May laughter and quirks be our only attempt!

Bracelet of Bravery

A bracelet I wear, it's flashy and bright,
It jangles and clinks, oh what a sight!
Proclaiming my bravery with each little jolt,
Yet sometimes it sparks when I'm flipping a bolt.

One day I decreed, 'I shall conquer my fears!'
The bracelet just laughed and rolled on with cheers.
'You want to climb mountains?' it teased with delight,
But first, don't forget to turn off the light!

I ventured to speak brave words on a dare,
But the words got tangled like my unruly hair.
The folks all around held their sides and they cried,
'This bravery's contagious!' as I wedged inside.

So now as I wear this glittery chain,
I embrace the missteps, the giggles, the pain.
For courage is laughter, and it's here to stay,
In my jingly bracelet, come join the fray!

Echoes of Empowerment

A trinket, a treasure, they say it inspires,
Yet mine does cartwheels, and laughs like a choir.
It echoes empowerment, but let's be real,
Most days we struggle, oh what a deal!

When wearing this charm, I stand oh so tall,
But slip on a banana, and I'm destined to fall.
While pretending to soar like a bird in the sky,
I end up just tumbling, feeling awfully spry!

Convinced I'm a hero, I march with great zeal,
Till a sneeze from a cat brings about my conceal.
'Empowerment's tricky!' I pat my own back,
As I leap over puddles, and aim for the crack!

In echoes of laughter, we find our true might,
So let's strut through the chaos, embracing the light.
For the gift of empowerment's wrapped in a joke,
And the silliest moments are truly bespoke!

The Serpent's Embrace

In a garden of glitter, a snake wears a grin,
Telling tales of the mischief, it's ready to spin.
With scales shining bright, it's a sight to see,
Whispering secrets of how to be free.

It slithers on coiling, with a laugh in its hiss,
Wonders what happens when you take a wrong twist.
Baffles the cats with its waggly tail,
Each wiggle a story, each wiggle a trail.

When tea time arrives, it curls up with glee,
Inviting the frogs for a cup of green tea.
Jokes on the lizards, all scaly and wise,
In the serpent's embrace, laughter multiplies.

A crown made of daisies, a cloak of fine twine,
This snake runs the circus, oh what a fine line!
Life's filled with giggles, with twists and with bends,
In the embrace of this snake, the fun never ends.

Legacy of the Luminary

A pebble once glimmered, they said it had flair,
Claimed it could dance, not a worry or care.
It taught the old rocks how to shine in the sun,
Hilarity bloomed, and the fun had begun.

This gravelly gem loved a good party, you see,
With sparks of laughter, it giggled with glee.
It wobbled on four legs like a baby in shoes,
Spreading bright joy like a jokester's muse.

Stars watched in envy, as it boogied around,
A legacy built on the silliest sound.
Who'd thought such a stone could dream of a show?
Where humor and glimmer formed quite the grand flow!

So come join the fun, let's twinkle and shine,
With our pebble of laughter, our spirits entwined.
It winks at the night, full of zest, cracking jokes,
With a legacy bright, as we dance with the folks.

The Watcher's Opal

A gem so round, with a mischievous glint,
It kept all the gossip, oh what a hint!
From marbles to muggles, it knew all the dirt,
Peeking through curtains in silence and mirth.

When shadows passed by, it giggled with ease,
Watching the clowns wrestle with pies and with cheese.
The neighbors all wondered who made that loud sound,
But the opal just chuckled, spinning giggles around.

In a world of whispers, it brought on the cheer,
With tales of the silly, it drew everyone near.
In a pyjama party, it twinkled with light,
A watchful companion, bringing joy in the night.

So raise up a toast to the round little stone,
A keeper of laughter, never alone.
Through secrets and stories, it'll always be there,
With a chuckle of wisdom and a secret to share.

Influence Encased

In a box full of baubles, one shone with a jest,
Full of bright colors, it felt like the best.
It winks at the onlookers, "Look at my flair!"
Casting silly shadows, bringing giggles to air.

When crowded with friends, it sparked up the fun,
A game of charades till the laughter was done.
This trinket of joy wore a crown made of jokes,
With each chuckle and grin, it delighted the folks.

A chatterbox treasure, it spun tales with ease,
Of dandy old dragons who danced in the breeze.
In its whimsical charms, all madness was tamed,
With every bright flicker, a new laugh was claimed.

So here's to the sparkles that bring on the cheer,
Influencing joy, making darkness unclear.
For in those small treasures, lies laughter indeed,
In influence encased, it's fun that we need.

The Radiant Artifact

In the midst of chaos, it shines so bright,
A gem that sparkles, a comical sight.
It grants its wearer a mischievous grin,
Who knew such magic could cause such a din?

With a wink and a nudge, it leads the way,
Turning dull moments to a laugh-filled fray.
A slide in the mud, a trip on the street,
All thanks to this trinket, oh what a treat!

It whispers sweet nothings, but oh what a tease,
With every new joke, it aims to appease.
A party on fabric, a riot on wear,
Who knew bravery could be found in a flair?

So wear it with pride, let the laughter unfold,
This radiant treasure, a sight to behold.
As we dance and we giggle, our spirits take flight,
With this charming bauble, every day's just right!

The Talisman of Valor

Deep in a drawer where odd socks reside,
There lives a strange charm, full of mischief and pride.
It transforms every task into a grand affair,
Even washing the dishes feels rarified air!

When wielded by fools with jest in their hearts,
It turns mundane moments into comedic arts.
Fighting fears, laughing loud at what's dur,
This magical oddity knows what to stir!

A coffee spill here, a tumble there too,
Each mishap becomes a story anew.
With a touch of humor and quirk on display,
The fellowship blossoms, it brightens the day!

So here's to the laughter this trinket bestows,
Turning daily routines to hilarious shows.
For courage is found not in battles or scars,
But in cracking a joke 'neath the light of the stars!

Crowned in Courage

A sparkly crown upon my head,
Making me feel like the queen, I am led.
It grants a silly swagger, an over-the-top stance,
Watch as I waddle and try for a dance!

With every step, the laughter erupts,
A spectacle it makes, as I trip and I thump.
Gather 'round, friends, this show's just begun,
Courage is messy, but oh, it's such fun!

Through puddles I splash, with flair and with style,
In the realm of the goofy, I'm queen for a while.
The bravest of knights would envy my glee,
For who else but me could this nonsense decree?

So pledge not your fealty, but chuckles instead,
In this crown of silliness, laughter is spread.
With joy in our hearts, we rally and cheer,
For the merry brigade shall conquer each fear!

The Empowered Pin

A pin that just twinkles, so simple, so sly,
It grants me a sparkle and catch in the eye.
With a flick of the wrist, it sets me apart,
But wait, what's this? A tickle to the heart!

It's not just a pin; it's a whimsical charm,
One pinch too close, it sets off alarm.
"Beware!" cries a friend as I prance through the room,
"My buddy's not brave, but it wreaks lots of doom!"

It guides all my ventures, both clumsy and bold,
Turning everyday mishaps to tales to be told.
With laughter erupting, I conquer the slight,
Is it magic or madness? Oh what a delight!

So when you feel down, wear this nifty little thing,
It reminds us to laugh, and our spirits will sing.
In the face of it all, remain lighthearted and true,
For joy is the power we all can imbue!

Virtue Encapsulated

In the heart of my blouse, it gleams with flair,
A sparkly thing, beyond compare.
It's said to bring luck, so I wear with pride,
But my cat thinks it's food, oh, how I hide!

With each little twinkle, it whispers my name,
I laugh as it dances, it's quite the game.
Yet every time I reach for my tea,
It rattles and rolls, oh, so carefree!

My friends all adore it, they beg me to share,
But truth be told, they're just after my flair.
For in this little gem, I find my might,
A laughable charm that shines so bright!

So here's to the sparkles, the giggles they bring,
I wear it with laughter; it reigns like a king.
Though it's just a trinket, it makes me believe,
That jokes and good fortune are all I need!

The Guiding Gemstone

Once I found a stone, shaped like a cat,
I thought it would guide me, imagine that!
With each tiny shimmer, it seemed so wise,
But led me to pizza, much to my surprise!

It sat on my collar, a fun little bling,
I told my best mate, "This will be the thing!"
But every direction led straight to food,
As if this old gem just wanted some dude!

I strolled with great pride, my compass so bright,
Yet every time it blinked, it felt not quite right.
To the nearest taco stand, it pulled my hand,
What a silly gem, it just loves the land!

So I keep it close, with a chuckle or two,
A guiding stone for a taco rendezvous.
It may not be wise, but delights my heart,
For laughter and tacos are the best kind of art!

The Relic of Resolve

Behold my relic, a magical piece,
It holds all my dreams, or at least, a few brie cheese.
With every good luck charm, it's quite the sight,
But why does it wiggle? Oh, what a fright!

At meetings it gleams, I pretend it's my brain,
But secretly hoping it'll wash off the pain.
My boss gives a nod, thinks I'm full of grit,
But inside I'm just wishing for a taco split!

As I reach for some wisdom, it clinks on the desk,
I tip it with style, like a bold burlesque.
It's really a joke, a humorous dance,
That leaves all my coworkers in a comical trance!

Though it may not be mighty, it holds my resolve,
My laughter and silliness, it helps me evolve.
For when life gets dull and the humor won't land,
I rub my small relic, it gives me a hand!

Crown of the Unyielding

Upon my head rests a crown made of flair,
It whispers of glory, but really, beware!
For inside its gold sparkles and dazzling sheen,
Lurks the fish I forgot, oh, what a scene!

"My majesty shines!" I declare with a grin,
While crumbs of good snacks tumble down from my chin.

It's a crown of great laughter by day or by night,
Though it's no royal treasure, it feels just right!

With every bold jest, it tilts on my brow,
Wobbling with laughter, it demands I bow.
The jester within me reigns ever so bold,
For a giggle-filled crown? That's the best kind of gold!

So wear a good laugh like a crown made of fun,
And may your heart flourish before the day's done.
For in every silly crown, there's laughter so sweet,
The essence of joy makes life feel complete!

Resilience in Reflections

In the mirror, a sparkle gleams,
Says, 'Hey there, I've got dreams!'
Dancing around with flair and style,
Come on now, let's laugh a while.

A twist of fate, a shiny claw,
Makes my ego feel like a law.
I strut like a peacock, proud and bright,
Chasing worries away—what a sight!

A playful wink from a glimmer consoled,
Turns my shy giggles into bold.
Every joke, a reflection's delight,
My charm is a riot, oh what a night!

With humor tucked beneath my sheen,
I tackle life like a quirky queen.
May the world keep spinning with playful cheer,
For laughter's truly my secret sphere.

Emblem of Might

In a world where tension rules the day,
   I wear my flair like a funny cliché.
With a wink and grin, I take my stance,
   Turning each wrinkle into a dance.

A badge of honor made from jest,
   Sparkling humor, I wear with zest.
When troubles strike like a rainy cloud,
   My laughter rings out, bold and loud.

I juggle stress like it's a fun game,
   With every chuckle, I rise to fame.
Chaos retreats when I make a quip,
In the sketch of life, I'm the funny clip.

So here's to the charm of a giggly might,
   Creating joy from the morning light.
I'll wear my laughter, my golden shield,
In the battle of life, it's the ultimate yield.

Ornament of Dominion

Glittering boldly on my chest,
This silly sparkler knows me best.
Like a crown of laughter, it reigns supreme,
Turning my frown into a silly beam.

With each jingle, I strut like a king,
Sharing giggles, what joy they bring!
In a kingdom where humor takes the throne,
I rule with glee; I'm never alone.

A comedic twist, I claim my ground,
Where smiles sprout and laughs abound.
No battle is lost with a playful quirk,
In this realm of joy, I am the perk!

So let the world know I wear my crown,
With humor and charm, I'll never frown.
In the parade of laughter, let's all unite,
As the ornament of bright delight.

The Jewel's Whisper

Oh, this tiny gem has quite the tale,
Whispers of fun in every gale.
It tickles my mind, makes spirits soar,
With a touch of laughter, who could want more?

As it twinkles warm, I spin around,
Dancing in rhythms of silly sound.
No worries allowed in this cheerful space,
The jewel spins light with giggly grace.

From worries to jests, it's quite the shift,
This playful trinket is a true gift.
Bringing joy like confetti in the air,
A reminder that laughter is truly rare.

So let's celebrate with this gem aglow,
With every chuckle, we let it flow.
In the echo of smiles, let dreams unfurl,
For a little jest can change the world!

The Crowned Essence

In a land where socks wore crowns,
And jellybeans ruled the towns,
A sparkly gem caught everyone's eye,
It whispered secrets, oh my, oh my.

A squirrel danced atop a cake,
Claiming that it was no mistake,
With laughter echoing all around,
Joy and silliness lost and found.

A parrot chattered in delight,
Wearing shades both day and night,
It fanned its feathers, flaunted the flair,
While giggles filled the sunlit air.

So here's to treasures, bright and bold,
With stories of mischief yet untold,
A glittering laugh in every clink,
You never know what gems might think.

Sigil of Strength

In a kingdom full of chocolate mice,
They chuckled, 'Strength comes at a price!'
With gummy bears as shields so sweet,
They hopped around on jelly feet.

A knight once wielded a licorice sword,
But it melted — oh, how he roared!
With every bite, his laughter grew,
As gummy foes just wobbled through.

A dragon sneezed, it was quite grand,
And out popped popcorn, in high demand,
They filled the skies with buttery fun,
As heroes danced, their battles won.

So remember, strength comes in tears,
Of laughter shared, not all our fears,
For in this realm of sugary might,
We find our joy, both day and night.

The Locket's Legacy

A locket once wore a tiny cat,
Who swore to sit upon the mat,
With tales of yarn and mice galore,
It sparked a quest for more and more.

A bunny peeked out from behind,
With carrots fresh, the best you'll find,
Its giggles echoed through the wood,
In hopping circles, life was good.

They struck a pose, in gleeful throng,
While singing silly kitten songs,
But wait! A locket tackled the floor,
And turned their tales to quest for lore.

So let it shine, this little gem,
With laughter spun like a bright diadem,
In every twist, a giggle waits,
As joy unlocks all of life's gates.

Embers of Conviction

In the forest where the squirrels play,
They plot their schemes from day to day,
With acorns flung and nuts in tow,
They spark the fires of friends in tow.

A wise old owl, with glasses thick,
Chortled at the woodland trick,
He spun a yarn of zest and cheer,
"A dance-off waits, all MUST be here!"

The raccoons pranced in shiny shoes,
While foxes brought elaborate clues,
They swept the leaves, a twirling dance,
With giggles booming, took their chance.

So gather 'round, let laughter grow,
In every ember, let it glow,
For conviction's gift is fun with friends,
Where giggles linger, laughter never ends.

The Ornament of Influence

In a drawer, it sparkles bright,
With mischief gleaming, what a sight.
It whispers secrets, oh so sly,
A butterfly that makes you fly.

It giggles when the neighbors prance,
And comes alive with every glance.
A wink can turn the onlookers' heads,
Transforming dullness into threads.

The cats all stare with envy keen,
As you adorn in silver sheen.
You strut about with subtle glee,
The life of parties, oh, that's me!

Scepters of Subtlety

A tiny trinket with a plan,
To rule the room, it takes a stand.
It jabs at fashion's lofty throne,
With laughs that echo, all alone.

A flick of wrist, a twirl of charm,
The crowd's amusement, like a balm.
It's just an object, meek and small,
Yet bids the world to laugh and brawl.

Its influence shapes a playful jest,
A subtle power, can you guess?
It winks at those who take it light,
Turning the mundane into flight.

Shimmering Command

A glimmer perched upon my chest,
It leads the way, who would have guessed?
With every shimmy, wiggle, sway,
It reigns supreme in a comical way.

Friends assemble, what's the fuss?
Oh, just the sparkles making us.
It gives us jests and silly puns,
A simple gem that just out-runs.

With laughter wrapped around its glow,
It brightens up the dreariest show.
Like magic wands in jest we dance,
In shimmering whims, we take a chance.

The Power in the Pin

Perched upon my jacket's seam,
A tiny beacon, holds a dream.
It puffs with poise, a little kin,
Commanding laughs as I begin.

It's just a pin, yet boasts of might,
A scepter forged in pure delight.
The fold of fabric, snug and tight,
Turns mundane moments into bright.

So joyfully I strut along,
With jesters' tunes, a silly song.
The power resting on my thread,
An artifact of laughs widespread.

The Seal of Sagas

In a land where tales do boggle,
A trinket sits, a grand old snoggle.
With every twist, it spills a yarn,
Of wise old goats and fields of corn.

It tickles tongues of knights and jesters,
Who spin grand tales of their conquests, besters.
No dragon slain or maiden's plight,
Just cats that dance in the pale moonlight.

The stories leap from lips like grass,
Every chuckle shared, a living mass.
With each retelling, laughter grows,
As the seal springs forth, mightier than prose.

So gather 'round and heed the call,
Of the laughing seal that knoweth all.
For every saga needs a cheer,
And this funny trinket brings good cheer.

Fragment of Fate

A piece of luck, a splintered chance,
Worn on a cloak, a quirky dance.
It wiggles and jigs with every twist,
Leaving all who see it in a fit.

In the market square, it starts to boast,
Of silly pranks and breakfast toast.
With every shout, the townsfolk grin,
This fragment makes them all dive in.

It twinkles bright like a starry night,
And guides the lost with laugh and light.
No serious fate can ensue with ease,
When fortune sparkles, everyone's at peace.

So tip your hats to this jesting shard,
For fate's a laugh, and it's never hard.
Embrace the goofs, the giggles and cheer,
With every chuckle, life's crystal clear.

The Celestial Brooch

A shiny pin from realms above,
Worn by a bee with dreams of love.
It buzzes tunes of a cosmic plan,
Making every flower twirl and stand.

While moonbeams giggle and sunbeams chime,
This dainty piece plays hopscotch with time.
With every flick, it spins a tale,
Of alien cows on a comet's trail.

The starlit sparks light up the night,
With silly jokes that take to flight.
No serious vibe can hold it tight,
As laughter bounces, oh what a sight!

So when you see the pin take flight,
Follow the buzz; it's pure delight.
For in the cosmos, the fun's the key,
With every giggle, we're wild and free!

The Ushering Stone

A pebble small, but oh so grand,
It rolls around and takes the stand.
With every nudge, it shows the way,
To ticklish jokes and a merry play.

It whispers secrets in a breeze,
Of dancing ants and jazzy bees.
No road is straight, no path is dull,
With this stone's help, the laughter's full.

It nudges feet towards the fun,
As rainbows pop out, one by one.
The world turns bright with every jest,
In its presence, all feel blessed.

So take a tip from that clever stone,
For humor's best when shared alone.
In giggles, grins, and silly cheers,
This ushering rock dispels the fears.

www.ingramcontent.com/pod-product-compliance
Lightning Source LLC
Chambersburg PA
CBHW051733290426
43661CB00123B/259